Think Again

Richard Chalon Aiken MD PhD

Lakeland Behavioral Health System

Go Ahead Publishing

2016

ISBN: ISBN-10: 0692702709
ISBN-13: 978-0692702703

Go Ahead Publishing
www.goaheadpublishing.com

Dedication

We dedicate this workbook to the many adolescents who inspired its creation and provided feedback through its many revisions. We think again and again about your success.

Actual and typical dialogue from an adolescent participant:

Dr. Aiken: *Congratulations on successfully completing your program.*

Adolescent: *Thanks!*

Dr. Aiken: *I understand that you have been using some special coping skills.*

Adolescent: *Yeah, my therapist has taught me Cognitive Behavioral Therapy and it really works for me.*

Dr. Aiken: *How does it work?*

Adolescent: *Well like a big trigger for me is when someone yells at me. That made me feel angry and sad because I thought everyone is down on me and I've had enough of it so I'd act up, yell back, curse, and get a bad attitude. With CBT, I tell myself I'm okay, they are the one who's got something going on right now, not me. Then I feel good that I can control myself. I think everybody should use it; I'm going to teach it to my mom when I get home!*

Preface

We are delighted to offer this workbook as a simple effective approach to alleviating emotional challenges faced by many adolescents and young adults.

The technique employed is that of Cognitive Behavioral Therapy (CBT), generally accepted as a best therapeutic practice for children, adolescents, and adults experiencing a variety of life distresses. As we discovered, there was a lack of available suitable instruments to utilize this technique for adolescents in group or individual therapy, therefore "Think Again" was created.

Briefly, CBT recognizes that the human condition is influenced by a series of triggers that through conditioned responses, leads to emotions, some of which may be unpleasant and may result in undesirable behavior. However, if we think again after such triggers until our emotions are more acceptable, this can result in more acceptable behavior.

We have utilized this workbook in various revised versions over the past dozen or so years in both in-patient and residential settings on thousands of adolescents with great success and, therefore, wish to offer it to therapists, parents, and adolescents in all settings.

There are five Chapters. Each may be used in one session, for example one each weekday for five settings. It is important for the participant to internalize the content of each Chapter before moving on to the next. Once the workbook is completed, the real work begins: applying these concepts to everyday life.

The Appendix contains some additional "Think Again" concept workbook sheets. Eventually the idea is to not require this formal written procedure but instead process mentally. After considerable practice, this should become second nature.

We also offer a Think Again manual intended primarily for the adult facilitating therapy titled "Think Again: Therapist Instruction Manual". A related text also available to the general public after more than a decade of development, is the application of these techniques in the day-to-day, hour-by-hour setting at home or in any structured setting, titled "The Cognitive Milieu".

It is our sincere intent that this tried-and-true product will relieve some suffering and, indeed, elevate emotional wellness in our adolescents well into adulthood.

Richard C. Aiken, M.D., Ph.D.
Medical Director Lakeland Behavioral Health System
May, 2016

Chapter 1

This Workbook is Useless

This sign means an important point to think about again.

It really is. Only after you read it and study it and use it can it be helpful to you. Depending upon your thinking, it may be that what's in this workbook will help you become more happy more often. How much it helps depends totally on you and your willingness to think, and think again.

In fact, like this book, most everything has no particular meaning to you until you think about it and put meaning onto it. Consider germs, for example, you know - the creepy crawlies. You probably think of germs as bad, period. But some types of germs, certain bacteria, live in our bodies by the millions and are really important to our health. When you think about that, not all germs are bad after all.

1

As another example of how we put meaning onto stuff by our thoughts, consider a song. The first time you hear the song you might not like it that much, but after a while it might remind you of a person or something that happened while you heard it.

So then the song may have some special meaning to you resulting in feelings that are good, bad, sad, mad, glad - whatever. YOU create the meaning.

The table below lists a few other examples of things that you might think of as good or bad, depending on your point of view. For each example, **write down** if you think it is good or bad and why you think that.

example	good, bad?	Why?
broccoli		
pain		
school		
money		
chores		

There are no right or wrong answers in filling-out the table but there are several different ways of looking at each example. Some may see the example as a good thing and some may see it as not so good. Some ways of looking at each that is positive include: broccoli is healthy; pain is protective; school opens opportunities; money helps us survive; and doing chores teaches us responsibility.

Your ~~WorkBook~~ Playbook

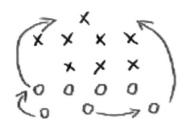

Okay, so let's start now to look at things in a positive way. Lets think of this "work"book as a "play" book instead - that we can have fun with this! In fact, it is very much literally a "playbook" in the sense that you have playbooks for various sports that help you pick out what to do when.

> *There is nothing either good or bad, but thinking makes it so.*
>
> - William Shakespeare,
>   Hamlet, Act 2, Scene 2

Now ... you have seen that there are lots of ways of looking at something. As we shall see in the following story, some ways lead to good feelings and some to not so good feelings.

The Tater Patch

Once upon a pretty long time ago, at a far-out place, there was a potato field warmed by the summer sun, fed by the rich soil, and watered by the plentiful rainfall. All of the splendid spuds were happy and healthy, if not wise. They could hardly be very wise as they had no contact with the real world, no ability to hear, see, touch, smell, or taste. But at least they thought they were happy, and so they were.

Then one day, something eye-opening happened - the taters sprouted eyes! Each potato could now see many magnificent sights such as dirt, stems, and, roots. And of course each other.

As the taters were looking around, it happened that they spotted the sun and this hurt their eyes. One such tater, called "Aggie - tater", had the half-baked thought that the sun was bad because of this; so she kept an eye on it – or three or four – because she was worried about what it might do next (this of course caused her to feel even worse).

4

Seeing this, her friend Emma-tater did likewise.

Hezie-tater wasn't sure about all of this at first, but eventually followed along with her two friends, as did most of the Spec-taters.

But Sweet-tater, a very smart spud, thought differently:

"This bright ball in the sky hurts my eyes, but only if I stare at it. I don't know what it is, but when it is gone I can't see anything at all, so maybe it is a good thing that it is there. I don't really know for sure if it is good or bad but when I think it is bad, I feel bad; when I think it is good, I feel good. So I'll just look on the bright side, eye think."

Well, it came to pass that Sweet-tater prospered and grew in size and sweetness, leading her partners in the patch to thoughts of envy and ever more distress.

But every year after that and to this very day, if taters aren't harvested in time and eaten, they'll sprout eyes, and lose their sweetness. But now sweet potaters don't get eyes at all yet get sweeter with time.

(In another part of the field, the corn grew ears but, shucks, that's another int-ear-esting but corny story.)

Comment-tater

If you were a tater in the patch, what kind of tater would you be and why do you say so? Please fill out:

Tater Type	Are you like this Tater Type (Yes or No)?	Why Do You Say That?
Aggie-tater		
Emma-tater		
Hezie-tater		
Spec-tater		
Sweet-tater		

Why were some of the taters unhappy about the sun?

How did Emma-tater feel about the sun?

How did Sweet-tater feel about the sun?

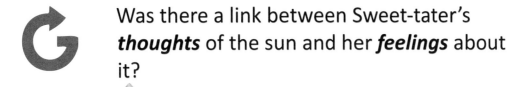

Was there a link between Sweet-tater's *thoughts* of the sun and her *feelings* about it?

What about such a link for the other taters?

Do you think it was better that they had eyes or not? Why?

Chapter 2

Trigger Happy

In Chapter 1, recall that when the taters saw the sun, it got them thinking. Sweet-tater noticed that when she thought good (positive) thoughts, she felt good; but when she thought bad (negative) thoughts, she felt bad. She was smart to make the decision to think the good way.

Trigger

↓

Thoughts

The sun was a "trigger"; it was something that they saw that then led to thoughts.

The sun was seen by Sweet-tater using her sense of sight; her brain then had two types of thoughts. Some were positive thoughts and some were negative thoughts.

Aggie-tater saw the sun too, but had thoughts that were negative; so did Emma-tater and other taters in the patch.

Triggers can result from things you see or hear – even what you touch, smell, or taste. Anything that you can "sense" using your five senses can be a trigger.

Triggers in themselves are not necessarily good or bad. It's how you "look" at them (or how you hear, feel, smell, or taste them)

The taters had no such triggers before they were given the ability to notice things through the sense of sight. Each thing they saw might lead to a positive thought or might lead to some "**stinkin' thinkin'**".

The stuff the taters saw didn't change at all by the taters' new ability to see them, but the taters' thoughts did change.

> *Anyone can see a forest fire. Skill lies in sniffing the first smoke.*
>
> - Robert Heinlein

So triggers are things you sense that lead to thoughts.

Trigger

↓

Thoughts

↓

Emotions

Of course, although triggers can lead to thoughts that are positive or negative (or in-between), we are most concerned here about triggers that lead to negative thoughts because these often lead further to negative feelings and emotional distress.

Here is a list of some common triggers that can lead to emotional distress in some people. Please fill out the table below:

Trigger	Possible Negative Feeling
Peer calls you a name.	
You score low on an important test.	
Your parents ground you.	
You get in trouble for something you didn't do.	
Your best friend seems to reject you.	

Comment-tater

Let's say that one of your best friends is angry at you and states that he/she never wants to see you again. No explanation is given and that person will not talk with you about it.

How would you "look at" that? What might be your thinking?

How might you feel?

What might you do?

TATER Task

What are some things that "trigger" you? Please fill out the TATER Task on the next page with examples of triggers that lead you to think thoughts that are "negative" or unpleasant.

TATER Task

Chapter 3

It's the Thought That Counts

We saw in the last chapter that triggers can lead to negative thoughts that in turn can lead to bad feelings. In many cases these negative thoughts are not really helpful; in fact, they are frequently the result of incorrect or "***stinkin' thinkin'***."

Trigger

Thoughts

Emotions

The idea here is that if we can think correctly, we will avoid unnecessary bad feelings.

Often after a trigger the negative thoughts come into mind rapidly without much effort on our part, so called "automatic thoughts". We have been conditioned to have such thoughts through life experiences.

Let's explore now the nature of these automatic thoughts.

Automatic Thoughts

Automatic thoughts are self-statements that we usually say to ourselves in certain situations. They can be positive or negative. Problems can happen when these automatic thoughts are negative. They are automatic because they are not the result of careful thinking, they are a "knee-jerk" reaction to situations. For example, in social situations, do you assume that people dislike you, or don't accept you?

There are many types of automatic thoughts, some of which are given below.

All or Nothing: no grey or in-between; either all good or all bad; must be "my way or the highway".

Mind Reading: "knowing" what someone else is thinking, when this is not possible.

Magnification: "blowing things out of proportion"; "making mountains of mole hills".

Over-generalizing: for example, use of the words "always" and "never".

Catastrophising: assuming that "the world will end" if a certain outcome is not achieved.

Comment-tater

In the following table, write the name of the Automatic Thought Type illustrated by the example thoughts.

Thought	Automatic Thought Type
"I can never do anything right!"	
"They said they liked me but they didn't really mean it."	
"Anyone who calls me a name is going to get punched."	
"If that happens, I won't show my face in public again!"	
"If I can't be captain of the team, I'll quit."	
"I'm always getting in trouble."	

TATER Tales - Mashed TATER Tot

Chapter

Feeling Well

Think you know the difference between thoughts and feelings? Think again. What about the statement "I feel unappreciated?" or "I feel uncared for?". Those are thoughts, not feelings or emotions. Emotions include, as examples:

- Happy
- Sad
- Anxious
- Upset
- Content
- Angry
- Loving
- Lonely

When someone is "feeling unappreciated" they usually mean something like "I'm feeling sad" or "I'm feeling angry." Those emotions are a result of the thought that others don't appreciate us.

Thoughts are easier to change than feelings, and in fact changing our thoughts can change how we feel.

In the following table, break down the statements given on the left-hand side into a thought statement and a feeling statement.

Statement	Thought	Feeling
I feel in danger.	I'm in danger.	I'm scared.
I just felt like hitting him.		
I won't do my homework because I don't feel like it.		
I feel left out.		

Expressing Emotion: Response

Most strong emotions are expressed by some kind of action or behavior. Although thoughts and feelings are reversible, actions are not - and can lead to serious consequences. As we have seen, controlling your thoughts helps how you feel - THAT in turn can affect what you do.

The following table lists some possible thought - emotion pairs; for each write down a possible response.

Thought	Emotion	Possible Response
If I mess this up, it's all over!	**anxiety**	
I am a worthless failure.	**sadness**	
That person is the reason my life is miserable!	**anger**	
Don't you call ME stupid!	**upset**	

TATER Task

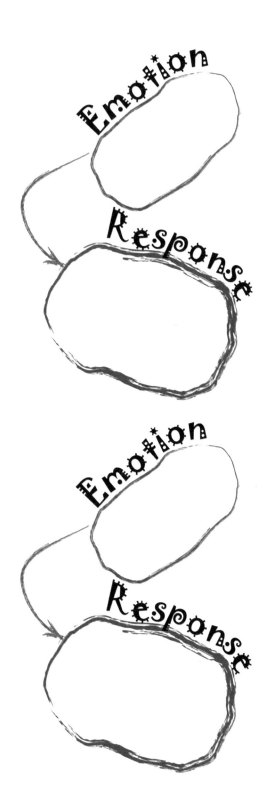

Emotion

Response

Emotion

Response

Have you ever used the excuse "*He made me mad*" for your negative behavior? While any feeling you might have is valid at the time, responses to those feelings that negatively affect others are not.

In the figures to the left, start with a negative behavior you may have used in the past, labeled "Response" and then recall your emotions just before that.

That's working backward from the direction of the arrow; so if in the past you, for example, cursed at someone, write under Response "cursed". Then think of how you felt just before cursing and write that under "Emotion"; perhaps the emotion was anger or hurt.

Thinking Again and Again

How many therapists does it take to change a light bulb? One, but it may take a lot of light bulbs!

Chapter 5

TATERs and ~~whirled peas~~ World Peace

Hey, we all need coping skills
I've been sliced and diced,
mashed and trashed - but I'm okay
cuz I have TATER Power!
In this Chapter you will put
everything you have already
learned in this workbook
together to help you make
good decisions, have good
feelings and good behavior.
Can you dig?

This is what I stand for:

T is for Trigger
Triggers can be big or small,
    good or bad or in-between.

AT is for Automatic Thought
This is the first thought that
comes into your head.

E is for Emotion
The way you feel follows the way
you think.

R is for Response
This is what actions you take, your
behavior.

TATER Task

Trigger

Choose a situation that has troubled you recently, find the trigger, and fill out this figure.

Thought

Emotion

Response

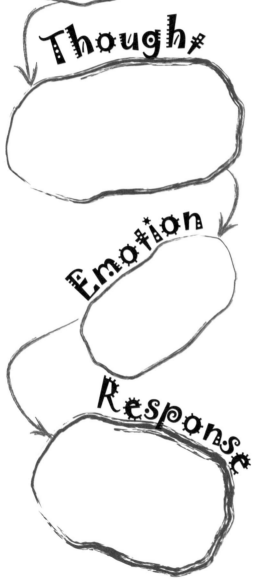

Want the Key to Happiness?

 Okay, it's **controlling your thinking**. Any negative thought, such as an automatic thought (AT) that follows a trigger (T), can lead to bad feelings or emotions (E) and possibly poor behavior (response, (R). Rethinking such thoughts can lead to more acceptable feelings and behavior.

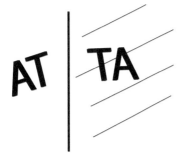 Let's reflect for a moment on the automatic thought, AT. If we actually reflect the letters AT in a mirror, what do you see? Why, you see the letters TA, that's what. TA stands for **Think Again** and that's exactly what you should do until your emotions are okay. If your emotions are okay, your response will probably be okay, too.

 So if an automatic thought, AT, gives hurtful feelings, you should think again, TA, until those feelings are okay.

Comment-tater

Below are listed some common triggers. For each trigger, write down in the second column an automatic thought that might first come to mind but results in a negative emotion; then in the third column a better thought.

Trigger	Automatic Thought	Think Again
Peer calls you a name.	*Nobody calls ME a name, I should call him a name back.*	*That name-calling is his poor behavior; it has no real meaning to me.*
You get in trouble for something you didn't do.		
You find out that a "friend" is spreading ugly rumors about you.		
You do poorly on an important test.		

29

TATER Task

Trigger

This summarizes the whole workbook. Take a trigger that leads to a negative emotion and then Think Again until the emotion is more positive. Then write your response.

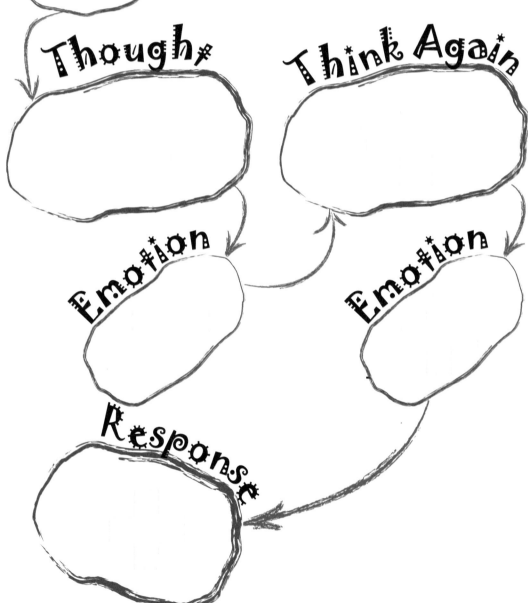

Thought

Think Again

Emotion

Emotion

Response

30

TATER Tales - Steamed Potatoes

© R.C.Aiken 2007

Appendix

Additional Think Again Worksheets

TATER Task

Trigger

This summarizes the whole workbook. Take a trigger that leads to a negative emotion and then Think Again until the emotion is more positive. Then write your response.

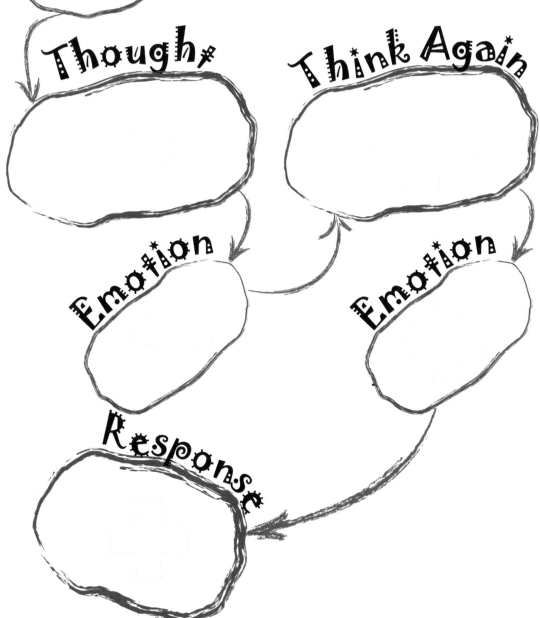

Thought

Think Again

Emotion

Emotion

Response

TATER Task

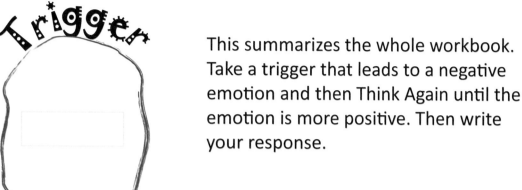

This summarizes the whole workbook. Take a trigger that leads to a negative emotion and then Think Again until the emotion is more positive. Then write your response.

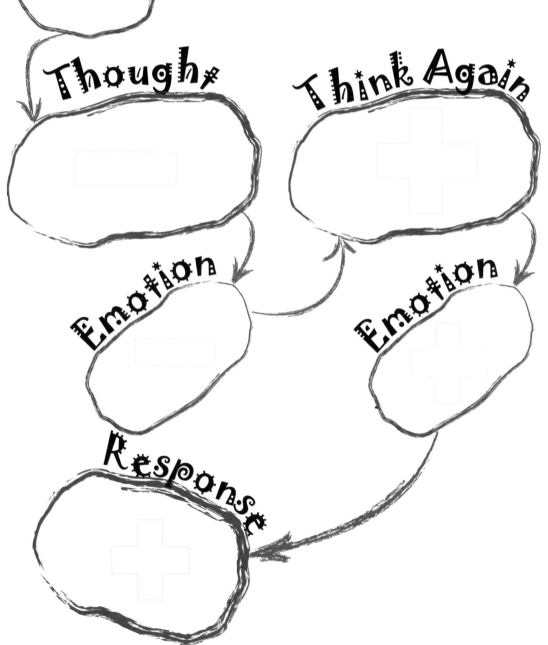

Trigger

Thought

Think Again

Emotion

Emotion

Response

TATER Task

Trigger

This summarizes the whole workbook. Take a trigger that leads to a negative emotion and then Think Again until the emotion is more positive. Then write your response.

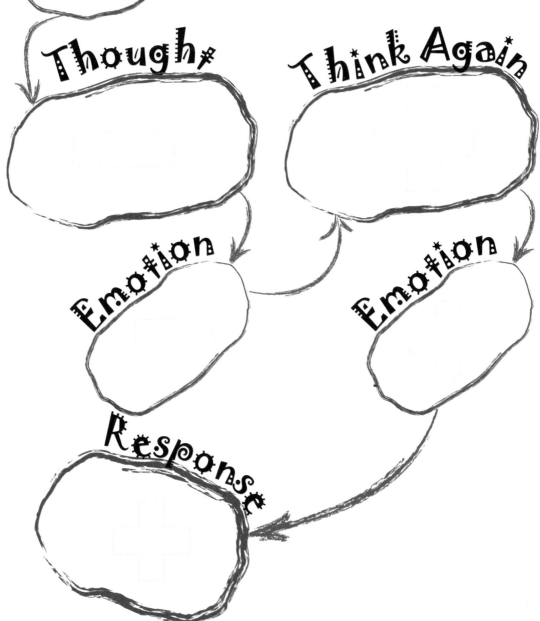

Thought

Think Again

Emotion

Emotion

Response

TATER Task

Trigger

This summarizes the whole workbook. Take a trigger that leads to a negative emotion and then Think Again until the emotion is more positive. Then write your response.

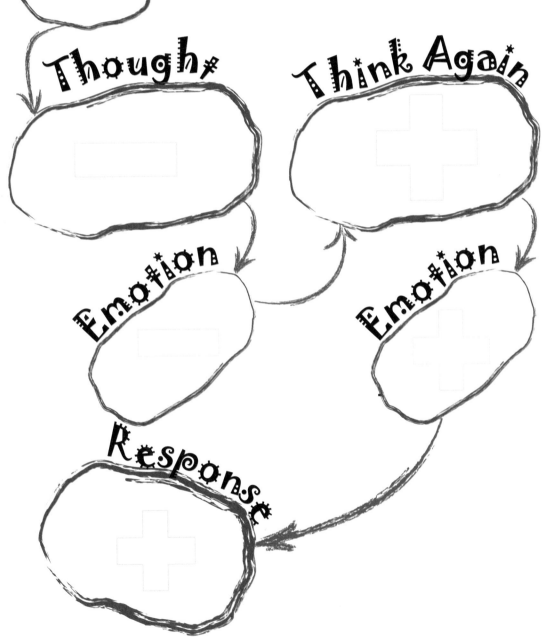

Thought

Think Again

Emotion

Emotion

Response

Made in the USA
Columbia, SC
23 February 2025

54297035R00027